Community Workers

# Keeping You Safe

## A Book About Police Officers

Ann Owen

Illustrated by Eric Thomas

Thanks to our advisers for their expertise, research, knowledge, and advice:

Officer James Caauwe, Bloomington (Minnesota) Police Department

Susan Kesselring, M.A., Literacy Educator
Rosemount-Apple Valley-Eagan (Minnesota) School District

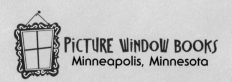

PICTURE WINDOW BOOKS
Minneapolis, Minnesota

Managing Editor: Bob Temple
Creative Director: Terri Foley
Editor: Peggy Henrikson
Editorial Adviser: Andrea Cascardi
Copy Editor: Laurie Kahn
Designer: John Moldstad
Page production: Picture Window Books
The illustrations in this book were prepared digitally.

Picture Window Books
5115 Excelsior Boulevard
Suite 232
Minneapolis, MN 55416
1-877-845-8392
www.picturewindowbooks.com

Printed in the United States of America.

Library of Congress Cataloging-in-Publication Data
Owen, Ann, 1953–
Keeping you safe : a book about police officers / written by Ann Owen ; illustrated by Eric Thomas.
p. cm. — (Community workers series)
Summary: Describes some of the things that police officers do to help keep people safe.
Includes bibliographical references and index.
ISBN 1-4048-0089-1
1. Police—Juvenile literature. [1. Police. 2. Occupations.]
I. Thomas, Eric, ill. II. Title. III. Community workers (Picture Window Books)
HV7922 .O9 2004
363.2'023—dc21
                                                                2003004165

Many people
in the community
have jobs helping others.

What do
police officers do?

A police officer teaches
us when to call 9-1-1

and to be careful around strangers.

What does your badge say?

# A police officer walks down the street

or drives a patrol car.

# Some police officers ride horses.

Some police officers teach bicycle safety.

I wear a helmet, too.

# Police officers work with partners.

Some police officers have
police dogs as partners.

Stay, Laser.

A police officer helps you if you get lost.

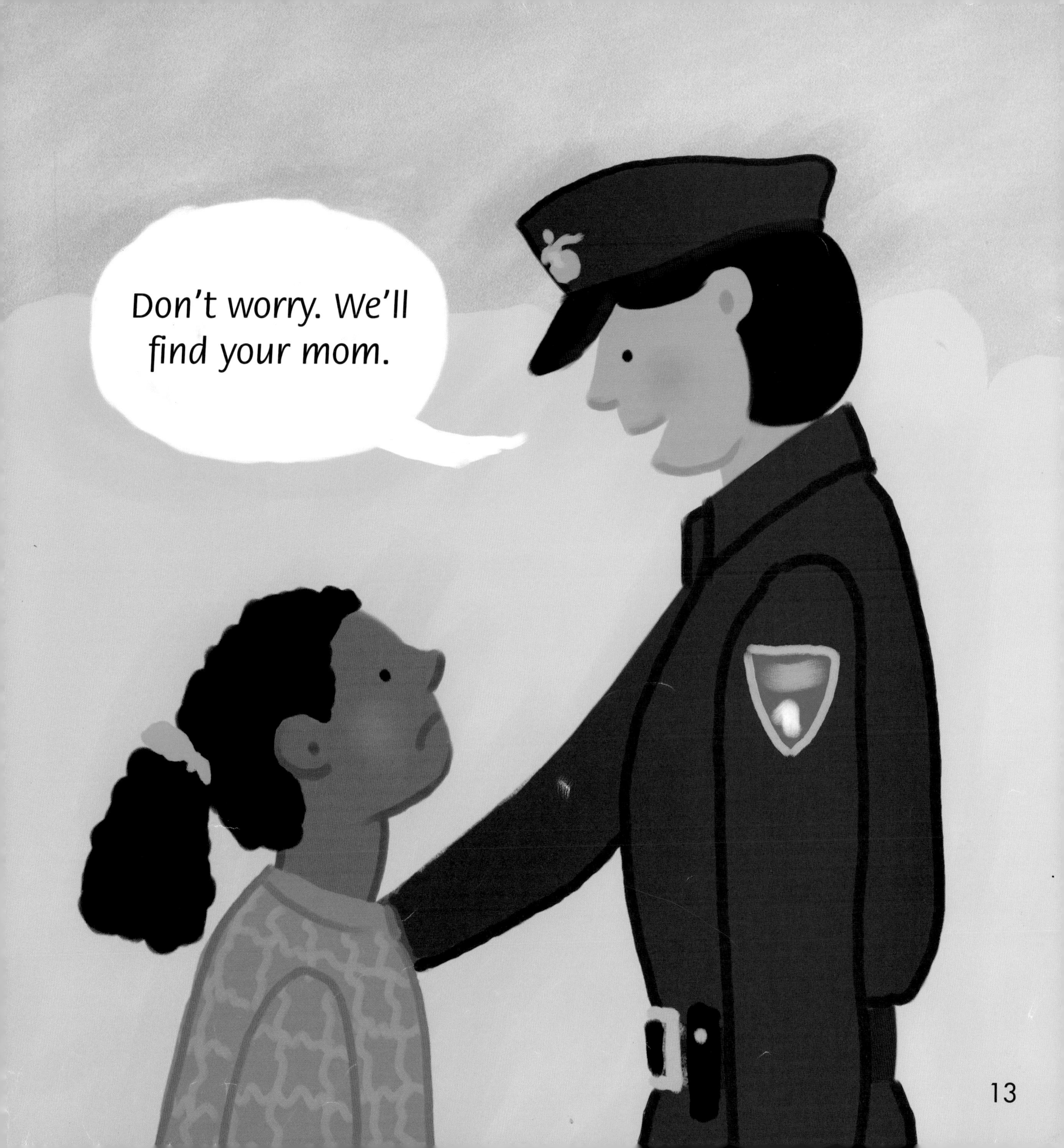
Don't worry. We'll find your mom.

A police officer makes
sure everyone is okay

and takes notes about what happened.

# Police officers look for clues.

17

A police officer speeds to the scene

and catches people who break laws.

Police officers help keep us safe.

# Did You Know?

- The first city in America to have a police force was Boston, Massachusetts. The force was started there almost 300 years ago.

- Boston, Massachusetts, and Chicago, Illinois, were the first cities in America where police officers wore uniforms.

- Lola Baldwin was the first female police officer. She joined the Portland, Oregon, police force almost 100 years ago.

- People disagree on the origin of the nickname "cop" for a police officer. Some think the name came from the fact that police badges used to be made of copper. Others say the name was created from the English term constable on patrol. A third opinion is that "cop" comes from a very old word that means to catch or capture.

- Police officers who work with police dogs are said to work "in K-9." This term comes from the word *canine,* which means having to do with dogs. *Canine* is pronounced like K-9.

# A Police Officer's Equipment

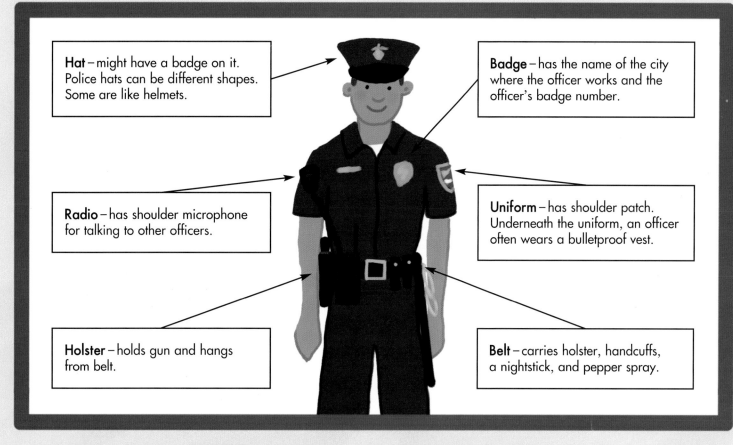

**Hat** – might have a badge on it. Police hats can be different shapes. Some are like helmets.

**Badge** – has the name of the city where the officer works and the officer's badge number.

**Radio** – has shoulder microphone for talking to other officers.

**Uniform** – has shoulder patch. Underneath the uniform, an officer often wears a bulletproof vest.

**Holster** – holds gun and hangs from belt.

**Belt** – carries holster, handcuffs, a nightstick, and pepper spray.

# Words to Know

badge (BAJ) – a small sign with a picture, name, or other information on it that is pinned to a person's clothing. Police badges are metal and may be different shapes. A police badge often looks like a shield.

community (kuh-MYOO-nuh-tee) – a group of people who live in the same area

fingerprint (FING-gur-print) – a print made by the pattern of lines on the tip of a person's finger. By checking for fingerprints at the scene of a crime, police officers can sometimes find out who committed the crime.

law (LAW) – a rule made by a government

patrol car (puh-TROLL KAR) – the car a police officer uses at work

pepper spray (PEP-ur SPRAY) – a spray that makes people's eyes itch. Police officers use pepper spray to protect themselves.

police force (puh-LEESS FORSS) – the group of police officers in a town or city

safe (SAYF) – free from harm

23

# To Learn More

## At the Library

Flanagan, Alice K. *Police Officers*. Minneapolis: Compass Point Books, 2000.
Hayward, Linda. *A Day in the Life of a Police Officer*. New York: Dorling Kindersley Pub., 2001.
Liebman, Daniel. *I Want to Be a Police Officer*. Toronto: Firefly Books, 2000.
Ready, Dee. *Police Officers*. Mankato, Minn.: Bridgestone Books, 1997.
Schaefer, Lola M. *We Need Police Officers*. Mankato, Minn.: Pebble Books, 2000.

## On the Web

**FBI Kids' Page**
For a virtual field trip at the FBI
http://www.fbi.gov/kids/k5th/kidsk5th.htm

**McGruff.org**
Safety tips, games, and online comic books
from the National Crime Prevention Council
http://www.mcgruff.org

**Fact Hound**
Want more information about police officers?
Fact Hound offers a safe, fun way to find Web sites related to this book.
All of the sites on Fact Hound have been researched by our staff.
http://www.facthound.com

1. Visit the Fact Hound home page.
2. Enter a search word related to this book,
   or type in this special code: 1404800891.
3. Click on the FETCH IT button.
Your trusty Fact Hound will fetch the best sites for you!

## Index